CW01472148

Original title:

In My Own Arms

Author: Eliora Lumiste

ISBN HARDBACK: 978-9908-1-2548-0

ISBN PAPERBACK: 978-9908-1-2549-7

ISBN EBOOK: 978-9908-1-2550-3

Wrapped in Soft Light

Twinkling stars above us gleam,
Laughter dances, like a dream.
Candles flicker, shadows sway,
Joyous hearts in bright array.

Colors burst, the night ignites,
As we gather, pure delight.
Warmth surrounds in every sound,
In this place, love's magic found.

Portrait of a Quiet Heart

In the hush of evening's glow,
Whispers of a soft hello.
Gentle songs begin to rise,
Serenity beneath the skies.

Bubbles pop and laughter flows,
Calmness in the joys that grow.
Time stands still in every beat,
Silent joy that feels so sweet.

Sanctuary within the Soul

Gathered close, a sacred space,
Smiles and warmth in each embrace.
Stories shared, our spirits blend,
In this moment, hearts transcend.

Candied treats and drinks to share,
Glow of joy is everywhere.
Underneath the starry dome,
Together here, we find our home.

The Music of My Own Breath

Breath by breath, the rhythm swells,
In my chest, a song that dwells.
Melodies of joy and cheer,
Every pulse, the world feels near.

Dancing shadows, lively nights,
Every heartbeat, sheer delights.
In this fest of love unbound,
Harmony is felt around.

A Gentle Harbor

Beneath the stars, the lanterns glow,
Laughter and music, hearts all aglow.
Colors of joy adorn the night,
In a gentle harbor, dreams take flight.

Friends gather 'round with smiles so bright,
Sharing warm stories, pure delight.
The breeze carries whispers, soft and low,
In this sanctuary, love can grow.

Cherished Solitude

In the quiet moments, joy resides,
Where laughter echoes, and hope abides.
A warm cup cradled, steam dancing high,
As dreams take shape beneath the sky.

The world slows down, in sweet embrace,
Finding solace in this cherished place.
A melody whispers through the air,
In solitude's arms, joy lingers there.

Within My Embrace

Wrapped in warmth, our hearts collide,
In a vivid dance, we laugh and glide.
Sparkles of joy in every glance,
Moments cherished, a sweet romance.

The world is bright when you're near me,
In every heartbeat, wild and free.
Together we weave a tapestry,
Of love and laughter, endlessly.

The Nest of My Thoughts

A cozy nook where dreams entwine,
Thoughts like feathers, soft and fine.
In the nest of hopes, colors blend,
Potent wishes, around the bend.

Whispers of joy fill up the air,
Ideas dancing, free from care.
In this warm space, my heart can soar,
Creating magic, forevermore.

The Heart's Quiet Refuge

In the glow of the lantern's dance,
Laughter weaves through the night air,
Families gather, hearts in trance,
Joy sparkles, a bright affair.

Under stars, the music swells,
Echoing dreams of yesteryear,
Whispers of love in gentle spells,
Together, we cast away fear.

Beneath the banners, colors gleam,
Sweets and smiles adorn the scene,
A tapestry of warmth, a dream,
In unity, we reign supreme.

With every cheer, the night ignites,
A canvas painted with delight,
Memories made in the soft moonlight,
The heart finds peace, a sweet respite.

Cradled in Stillness

In the hush of a winter's eve,
Soft snowflakes drift from the sky,
Candles flicker, and we believe,
That magic whispers, gently nigh.

With hands held warm, our voices rise,
In harmony, we find our grace,
A serenade beneath dark skies,
In this stillness, we embrace.

Hot cocoa warms our chilly toes,
Laughter bubbles like a stream,
Wrapped in love, the spirit grows,
Together, we weave our dream.

As stars twinkle like playful sprites,
Hope dances in the frosty air,
Cradled in warmth, our hearts take flight,
In stillness, we find what we share.

Embracing My Light

As dawn breaks with a golden hue,
I rise, ready to greet the day,
With open arms, my spirit true,
I embrace the joys that come my way.

In fields of laughter, I will roam,
Chasing dreams like butterflies,
With every heartbeat, I find home,
In every smile, my spirit flies.

Through rainy days, I'll dance and sing,
Finding beauty in every storm,
Each moment wraps me, a living spring,
In this journey, my heart stays warm.

Together we shine, a radiant crew,
In every gathering, bonds ignite,
With love's embrace, I am renewed,
Forever grateful, embracing my light.

A Hug from Within

In the glow of twinkling lights,
Joy dances with every heart,
Laughter floats like balloons,
A warmth that sets us apart.

Songs of cheer fill the air,
Crisp nights wrapped in delight,
Familiar faces all around,
The world shines a little bright.

Glistening dreams twirl and spin,
Festivities breathe life anew,
With every embrace we share,
Our spirits gleam like dew.

Celebration in every smile,
Together we weave our tales,
In the hug of joyous moments,
The essence of love prevails.

The Fortress of Self

Within these walls of joyful cheer,
My heart finds a radiant spark,
A fortress built through laughter,
Where dreams ignite in the dark.

Each corner bright with festive gleam,
Whispers of hope fill the air,
An inner peace, a soothing balm,
In this haven, we're all aware.

The spirit glows, in unity strong,
Together, we dance through the night,
Embracing all that life can bring,
Our fortress is bathed in light.

With every heartbeat, every cheer,
We weave our stories, bold and true,
In the fortress of love we share,
A tapestry of me and you.

My Personal Haven

Beneath the stars where laughter rings,
My haven bursts with delight,
Colors swirl like confetti dreams,
In this glow, the world feels right.

Soft shadows dance by the fire,
Messages of warmth unfold,
Every cherished moment glows,
In this haven, joy takes hold.

The scent of spice fills the air,
With friends who gather 'round,
Each tale told and hug exchanged,
In my haven, love is found.

Music plays, hearts intertwine,
With rhythm and laughter we blend,
In the sacred space we create,
Where every soul can mend.

Tenderness in Solitude

In the quiet of a gentle night,
I find my heart's sweet embrace,
A tender pulse, a lullaby,
In solitude, I touch grace.

Starlight whispers soft and low,
Each twinkle is a cherished friend,
In this stillness, I embrace,
The love within, that will not end.

The path of dreams illuminated,
With courage born from silence deep,
In this moment, I'm complete,
A joyful spirit, soothed to sleep.

Embracing all that life can give,
A festive heart within my soul,
In tenderness, I find my strength,
In solitude, I am whole.

Wrapped in Warmth

The fire flickers, shadows dance,
Laughter floats, a joyful chance.
Bright lights twinkle, hearts ignite,
In this moment, pure delight.

Cozy blankets, friends so dear,
Spreading love, spreading cheer.
Songs of joy, we all sing,
Wrapped in warmth, the joy we bring.

Cherished Whispers

Softest secrets shared tonight,
In the glow, everything feels right.
Stars above our heads do gleam,
Woven tightly, like a dream.

Lively chatter, soft and sweet,
Memories made, a lovely feat.
Tender moments, hearts entwined,
Cherished whispers, love defined.

Gentle Embrace of the Mind

In the quiet, thoughts take flight,
Dancing gently, pure delight.
With every breath, a sweet release,
Finding solace, finding peace.

Colors swirl in vibrant hues,
Creating worlds we cannot lose.
A gentle touch, a warm embrace,
In the mind's realm, a sacred space.

Alone Yet Complete

In solitude, the heart can sing,
Finding joy in little things.
Moments cherished, time well spent,
Alone yet complete, content.

The world outside may rush and race,
But here within, I've found my place.
Whispers of the soul's sweet grace,
Alone, I bloom, in my own space.

Dappled Shadows of Self

In the garden where laughter grows,
Colors dance in the evening glow.
Dappled whispers on the breeze,
Echoes of joy rustle the leaves.

Sunlight filters through the trees,
Casting shapes that tease and please.
In every corner, stories bloom,
Creating magic, dispelling gloom.

Children chase, their spirits free,
While petals fall, enchanting spree.
Time slows down in this bright space,
A celebration, a warm embrace.

A Soothing Embrace

Under the glow of soft lantern light,
Laughter flows like stars at night.
Gathering close, we share our tales,
In the warmth where every heart prevails.

Delicious scents waft through the air,
Wrapped in joy, we have not a care.
Fires crackle, the night takes flight,
In the embrace of love, everything feels right.

Voices blend in a harmonious song,
With every note, we feel we belong.
Together, we weave a tapestry bright,
In the soothing embrace of this festive night.

The Hug of Home

Open doors and smiles so wide,
Warmth and laughter here abide.
Every corner tells a story,
With the glow of everyday glory.

Familiar faces, bond so dear,
Each moment lived, our hearts adhere.
In the kitchen, aromas swirl,
Crafting joy in every whirl.

Passing stories, sharing dreams,
Life's simple pleasure endlessly gleams.
In this hug, all cares will roam,
Finding peace in the hug of home.

The Strength of My Silence

In the quiet of a festive night,
Stillness wrapped in soft moonlight.
Each unspoken thought, a treasure,
Whispers of joy, pure pleasure.

In moments spent, so rich and rare,
Silence holds a magic flare.
Where laughter dances, sparkles ignite,
In the strength of silence, hearts take flight.

Listening close, our spirits blend,
In the hush, our souls transcend.
Together we stand in peaceful chance,
In the strength of silence, we rejoice and dance.

A Portrait of Me

Colors bright, a brush in hand,
Laughter echoes, a joyous band.
Shapes of dreams in hues of delight,
A canvas filled with purest light.

Friends gather near, the warmth we share,
Dancing lights float through the air.
Every heart beat in harmony,
Together we create our symphony.

Moments captured, time stands still,
In this space, we feel the thrill.
With sparkling eyes, we paint the day,
In this portrait, we find our way.

As shadows fade, the sun will rise,
Beneath the sky, where joy denies.
Together we build, with love so free,
This vibrant life—a portrait of me.

The Safe Harbor Within

In the storm's eye, I find my rest,
A warm cocoon, my soul's behest.
Gentle waves lap, whispers low,
In this harbor, my spirit will grow.

Golden rays break through the gray,
Here, worries wash away in play.
Laughter dances on the breeze,
In this haven, my heart finds ease.

Companions gather, sharing dreams,
Under starlit skies, we weave our themes.
Joy ignites like fireflies bright,
In unity, we embrace the night.

Safe within this warmth we find,
A harbor true, where hearts unwind.
In every heartbeat, love's gentle spin,
We'll sail together, safe within.

The Nourishment of Solitude

In quiet corners, I take my time,
Nature's whispers, a soothing rhyme.
The stillness wraps like a tender sheet,
In this space, my heart finds beat.

Days drift by, a gentle flow,
In silent moments, my spirit grows.
Breath by breath, I soak it in,
Each thought a seed, new life begins.

The world outside fades to a hush,
In solitude's arms, I feel the rush.
Guided by peace, I find my way,
In nurturing stillness, I choose to stay.

With every pause, I gather strength,
In this sanctuary, I find my length.
So here I linger, heart open wide,
In solitude's grace, I take my stride.

Serenity's Whisper

In twilight's glow, soft shadows blend,
A calming breeze, where moments mend.
The stars emerge, a shimmering sweep,
In this stillness, my spirit's deep.

Crickets sing a lullaby sweet,
Guiding dreams on gentle feet.
Nature's embrace, a soothing balm,
In serenity's arms, I find my calm.

With every sigh, the world's refrain,
Fades into whispers, ease the strain.
Moonlight dances upon the stream,
In this stillness, I dare to dream.

Serenity's path leads me home,
In quiet love, I freely roam.
A heart at peace, forever shall,
Be wrapped in whispers, soft and small.

Embracing Solitude

In the golden glow of a setting sun,
I sip on joy, as the day is done.
Laughter whispers through the trees,
While gentle breezes sing with ease.

A canvas painted with vibrant hues,
Each moment sparkles, a sweet muse.
Festive lights twinkle in the night,
Embracing solitude, a pure delight.

Stars above dance like cheerful sprites,
Guiding my heart with playful lights.
In this silence, I find my song,
Embracing solitude where I belong.

Gathered moments, warm and bright,
Cocooned in peace, wrapped up tight.
With every breath, the world feels new,
Embracing solitude, as dreams ensue.

Cradling My Shadow

In the moonlit night, shadows play,
Cradling dreams as they sway.
With laughter echoing through the air,
Whispers of secrets drift without a care.

I dance alone on this festive floor,
Embracing all that life has in store.
With every twirl, my spirit soars,
Cradling my shadow, it ever adores.

Bright colors swirl like a painter's brush,
In this joyful moment, I feel the hush.
Cradling my shadow as a friend, it's true,
Together we wander, forever anew.

Underneath the stars, we share our glee,
In this dance of life, it's just you and me.
With a heart so light, my joy shall grow,
Cradling my shadow, I'm never alone.

Within My Grasp

A festive cheer fills the lively air,
With friends beside, we shed all care.
The music swells, and voices rise,
Laughter blooms like bright blue skies.

Within my grasp, the moments shine,
Every smile shared, a love divine.
Joy envelops like a warm embrace,
In this celebration, we find our place.

Chasing twilight, we follow the light,
Dancing together into the night.
With every heartbeat, our spirits gleam,
Within my grasp, we weave a dream.

The world spins on in joyous flight,
Together we bask in this beautiful night.
With every memory soft as a feather,
Within my grasp, we thrive together.

A Cocoon of Reflection

In twilight hues, I find my peace,
A cocoon of reflection, a sweet release.
Surrounded by laughter, joy takes flight,
In this festive moment, everything feels right.

The warmth of hearts, all intertwined,
Every shared glance, a joy defined.
Bubbles of laughter filled with light,
A cocoon of reflection, pure and bright.

With stars above, twinkling like dreams,
The world is a canvas of vibrant schemes.
In this embrace, I feel alive,
A cocoon of reflection, where hopes thrive.

Celebrations fill the glowing night,
With every pulse, the spirits ignite.
In this sacred space, love springs free,
A cocoon of reflection, just you and me.

Warmth in Silence

In the glow of candlelight, so bright,
Laughter dances, taking flight.
Smiles and whispers fill the air,
As love wraps us in its care.

Joyous hearts in soft embrace,
Finding magic in this place.
Songs of cheer begin to rise,
Echoing love beneath the skies.

Imagined dreams twinkle and gleam,
Woven together like a dream.
Hands held tight against the chill,
In this moment, hearts are still.

Celebration spills like wine,
Each story shared, a sign.
Together, we paint the night,
In warmth and silence, pure delight.

Reflection's Embrace

Mirrored faces, joy revealed,
In each heart, stories sealed.
Candles flicker, shadows play,
Guiding us along the way.

Time drifts softly, moments blend,
Old memories, kindness send.
A dance of light, the world transforms,
In reflection's embrace, the spirit warms.

Twinkling lights on every tree,
Whispers of love set us free.
Together, we cherish the past,
Holding onto moments that last.

Softly woven tales unfold,
In laughter, the warmth we hold.
With every smile, every cheer,
We gather close, our vision clear.

A Symphony of My Soul

In every note, a sweet refrain,
A melody that breaks the chain.
Harmony dances in the night,
As hearts unite in joyous flight.

Strings of laughter, drums of cheer,
Fill the air, revere the year.
Each tone a hug, each chord a kiss,
In this symphony, we find bliss.

Voices rise in songful grace,
The world fades, leaving just this space.
Under stars, our dreams take flight,
Wrapped in magic, hearts alight.

In the rhythm, we belong,
Together, we create our song.
A celebration of the whole,
In every beat, the soul's control.

Quiet Courage

In the shadow, courage stands,
Gentle heart and open hands.
Facing fears, we find our way,
In the quiet, courage stays.

Softly spoken, words of light,
Encouragement ignites the night.
Together we rise, bold and free,
Facing storms, just you and me.

Brave thoughts echo in our heart,
Each moment we play our part.
Through the trials, joy finds space,
In quiet courage, we embrace.

With every step, we choose to shine,
In the stillness, love entwines.
A dance of strength, a whispered cheer,
Together, we'll conquer each fear.

Nestled in Serenity

In the warmth of golden light,
Laughter dances in the air,
Colors bloom in pure delight,
Joyful hearts beyond compare.

Gathered round with songs to sing,
Friendship sparkles in the sun,
Every moment's offering,
Together, we are truly one.

Glimmers twinkle in the night,
Festive spirits, shining bright,
All worries fade out of sight,
In love's embrace, we take flight.

Let the stars our dreams ignite,
Whispers of the softest cheer,
In this peace, we feel so right,
Nestled close, we hold all dear.

The Comfort I Carry

A cozy fire flickers near,
In the glow, our laughter swells,
Memories dance, forever clear,
Enchanting tales, our hearts retell.

With every treat upon the plate,
Sweetened moments, rich and bright,
Happiness, we celebrate,
In each hug, there's pure delight.

Banners wave with joy and pride,
In unity, our spirits soar,
Together, with love as our guide,
We find comfort, evermore.

With every smile, our worries fade,
In this warmth, we dare to dream,
No greater bond can be made,
In the comfort of our beam.

My Heart's Gentle Hold

Under stars that softly gleam,
The night unfolds its gentle touch,
In this moment, love's sweet dream,
My heart's gentle hold means so much.

With family gathered close tonight,
We share stories, laughter flows,
Wrapped in love, the world's alright,
In this warmth, all friendship grows.

The sound of music fills the air,
A melody like honey flows,
Underneath the moonlit glare,
Our joyful spirits brightly glow.

In every hug, the world feels right,
The bonds we share, delicately spun,
Together, we embrace the night,
In my heart's hold, we are one.

Breath of Quietude

In the stillness of the twilight,
With fireflies weaving through the strife,
Voices blend in soft delight,
A breath of quietude in life.

Here beneath the whispering trees,
We find solace, pure and clear,
Every sigh a gentle breeze,
In this haven, love feels near.

As the stars begin to gleam,
Each moment wrapped in soft embrace,
Together weaving every dream,
In this space, we find our place.

With laughter's echo in the night,
Hearts entwined in purest song,
Our spirits soar, a joyous sight,
In breath of quietude, we belong.

The Comfort of My Soul

In the glow of twilight's grace,
Laughter dances, time slows its race.
Candles flicker, whispers of cheer,
Embracing each moment, holding it near.

Beneath the stars, hearts come alive,
Joyous melodies, like bees, they thrive.
Together we gather, love fills the air,
Memories crafted, with utmost care.

With every toast, our spirits soar,
In this warm circle, we yearn for more.
The comfort of souls, so sweetly shared,
In the festival of life, we're truly rare.

As dawn approaches, the night will fade,
Yet the laughter remains, forever made.
In every heartbeat, a story to tell,
In the comfort of my soul, all is well.

Unveiling Inner Light

Beneath the moon, a silver sheen,
The heart awakens, pure and keen.
In every smile, a spark ignites,
Unveiling inner light, through joyful nights.

Dancing shadows flicker and play,
As dreams emerge, in bright array.
With each step, the spirit sings,
Celebrating all the hope that spring brings.

Gathering moments, like stars in the sky,
Radiant whispers, as time floats by.
The joy we share, a vibrant glow,
In this festive dance, our spirits flow.

Together we shine, in colors so bright,
Embracing each other, hearts full of light.
In this wondrous realm, we find our might,
Unveiling inner light, a beautiful sight.

Serenity's Caress

Breezes whisper through trees so tall,
Nature hums a peaceful call.
In golden hues, the sun descends,
Serenity blooms, as day gently bends.

With every heartbeat, a tranquil song,
In this calm space, where we belong.
Soft laughter mingles with the breeze,
Wrapped in warmth, the soul feels at ease.

Time slows down, like shadows at play,
Every worry fades, drifting away.
Together we cherish, this moment's bliss,
In serenity's caress, we find our kiss.

As stars awaken, the night ignites,
In soothing silence, the heart takes flight.
In this embrace, we'll forever stay,
Serenity's caress, leading the way.

Finding Peace in Stillness

In the quiet of dawn, a promise unfolds,
Whispers of peace in memories gold.
With gentle eyes, we savor the view,
Finding peace in stillness, as morning breaks through.

The world around hums in soft tune,
A tranquil heart cradles the moon.
In the stillness, we gather and breathe,
With every moment, our worries we leave.

Hand in hand, we walk this path,
Sharing our laughter, embracing the math.
In the silence, connections deepen,
Finding peace in stillness, a love we've weakened.

As the sun rises high, we lift our gaze,
In this gentle calm, our spirits blaze.
With hearts intertwined, we dream and instill,
Finding peace in stillness, a joy to fulfill.

Garden of Dreams

In the garden bright and fair,
Colors dance in warm sunlight.
Joyful hearts together share,
Laughter sparkles, pure delight.

Flowers bloom in every hue,
Whispers of the breezy song.
Memories made, both old and new,
In this place where we belong.

Children play, their voices ring,
Butterflies flit through the air.
Hope and magic, what they bring,
Promises of love laid bare.

As the sun begins to set,
Stars awaken, bright and clear.
In this moment we forget,
All our worries, gone, no fear.

In the Arms of Reflection

Mirrors of the soul reveal,
Glimmers of what's deep within.
Under starlit skies we heal,
Finding peace where dreams begin.

Each thought flows like a gentle stream,
Washing over worries past.
In the silence, we may dream,
Moments crafted, meant to last.

With each breath, a new embrace,
Feelings intertwined with light.
In this space, we find our place,
Guided by the soft moonlight.

Hands held close, our spirits soar,
In the arms of dreams we grow.
In reflection, we explore,
Love's own magic, here, aglow.

A Serene Refuge

Nestled within nature's arms,
Whispers of the forest call.
Awash in beauty and its charms,
Echoes of peace gently fall.

Golden leaves swirl in the breeze,
Sunlight dapples on the ground.
In this stillness, hearts find ease,
In this haven, joy is found.

Birdsongs weave a melody,
Filling the air with sweet cheer.
For in this lush serenity,
Every moment feels so near.

Tucked away, our worries shy,
With each breath, a fresh new start.
In this refuge, we can fly,
Finding solace in the heart.

The Aroma of Self-Love

Scented blooms fill up the space,
Inviting us to breathe it in.
In this moment, find our grace,
With every heartbeat, we begin.

Lavender and rose entwined,
Whispers soft, like gentle rain.
In this fragrant world, we find,
A balm for all our hidden pain.

With each note, our spirits rise,
A symphony of sweet embrace.
In the silence, truth replies,
Self-love written on each face.

As we bask in this perfume,
Time slows down; we come alive.
In this space, we shed our gloom,
And with love, we surely thrive.

Embrace of Solitude

In the corner, soft light glows,
Whispers of joy, the quiet grows.
A dance with shadows, laughter near,
In solitude's embrace, we cheer.

Golden moments on a silver sea,
Time stands still, just you and me.
With every heartbeat, magic spins,
In this stillness, the festivity begins.

Joy flickers in the evening air,
Balloons float high, without a care.
Echoes of smiles, the heart does race,
In treasured stillness, we find our space.

As stars align, the night ignites,
Every glance, a spark of delights.
Together, we rise, together, we soar,
In this embrace, we seek evermore.

The Warmth of Solitude

In a cabin, the fireplace shines,
Flickering flames, tales intertwine.
The aroma of cocoa lifts the soul,
In solitude's warmth, we feel whole.

Outside, the world sparkles with cheer,
Inside, a haven where dreams appear.
Each sip of joy fills the room,
In a cozy cocoon, there's no gloom.

Delightful laughter drifts on the breeze,
Moments of magic put hearts at ease.
Glowing embers, dancing light,
In solitude's warmth, everything feels right.

So let the world whir outside loud,
Here in our haven, we feel proud.
With every heartbeat, happiness hums,
In this warm space, the festivity comes.

A Sanctuary of One

Nestled softly, my haven calls,
Where sunlight streams and shadow falls.
Within these walls, my spirit sings,
In this sanctuary, joy takes wing.

Whispers of nature through open air,
The rustling leaves, a gentle pair.
Moments unfold, embrace the views,
With each heartbeat, the warmth renews.

A tapestry woven from colors bright,
Festive dreams dance in the light.
Here in my space, all feels divine,
In this solitude, the stars align.

Cradled by silence, my heart does swell,
In this sanctuary, all is well.
With every moment, the spirit plays,
In solitude's joy, I spend my days.

Holding My Essence

In soft twilight, I find my peace,
Glimmers of hope that never cease.
Holding my essence, a spirit so bright,
In solitude's glow, I feel the light.

Colors swirl in a vibrant dance,
Each moment whispers a golden chance.
In laughter and cheer, life unfolds,
With every heartbeat, my story's told.

Embracing the quiet, I rise with glee,
In a world of wonder, I am free.
Shadows and dreams, hand in hand,
In solitude's magic, together we stand.

As nightingale sings, the stars align,
Holding my essence, everything's fine.
Within this bubble of festive glow,
In solitude's warmth, love begins to flow.

Portrait of Self-Acceptance

In the mirror, a smile beams bright,
Colors of joy glow in the light.
Embracing the flaws, I find my muse,
In the canvas of life, I gladly choose.

Stripes of laughter, dots of grace,
Every blemish, a cherished trace.
With a heart wide open, I stand tall,
In this masterpiece, I feel it all.

A swirl of dreams, a dash of hope,
I dance with shadows, learning to cope.
Each stroke whispers, 'You are enough,'
In the journey ahead, I rise above.

So here I am, both strong and free,
In the portrait of self, I truly see.
A tapestry woven with threads of cheer,
In acceptance, I find my frontier.

A Dance with My Essence

Twinkling lights above me swirl,
In this moment, my spirit unfurl.
With every beat, my heart takes flight,
A dance with my essence, pure delight.

Flickering candles cast a warm glow,
In the rhythm of life, I sway slow.
Whispers of nature sing in my ear,
Inviting me softly to hold dear.

Colors of laughter paint the air,
With each gentle turn, I cast away care.
In the embrace of the joyous night,
I twirl with my dreams, my soul ignites.

Under the stars, I find my beat,
In this waltz of self, life is sweet.
With joy as my partner, I freely glide,
In the dance with my essence, I reside.

The Refuge of Quiet Hearts

In a garden where silence blooms,
Whispers of peace chase away glooms.
Each gentle breeze carries a song,
In this refuge, we all belong.

Under the shade of ancient trees,
Laughter dances upon the breeze.
A haven created from dreams and care,
With every heartbeat, love fills the air.

Soft petals fall, a gentle grace,
In each moment, time finds its place.
With open arms, we gather near,
In the quiet haven, we hold dear.

Together we find solace and glow,
In the refuge where calm rivers flow.
With hearts entwined, we gently start,
In the safety of quiet hearts.

In the Arms of Comfort

In the cocoon of soft embrace,
I find my haven, a sacred space.
With every whisper, worries take flight,
Wrapped in warmth, bathed in light.

Gentle shadows dance around me,
In the stillness, I am set free.
With laughter echoing like a song,
In the arms of comfort, I belong.

Familiar laughter twirls in the air,
In each heartbeat, love lays bare.
With open hearts, we weave the night,
In this sweet solace, all feels right.

Together we share, together we dream,
In a tapestry woven, our spirits gleam.
In the embrace of joy, no fear to roam,
In the arms of comfort, I feel at home.

Rocking My Inner Child

Bubbles rise with giggles bright,
Colorful dreams taking flight,
Laughter dances in the air,
Joy awaits, a treasure rare.

Whirling 'round in blissful play,
Chasing worries far away,
Imagination paints the scene,
Innocence reigns, pure and keen.

Skipping stones on a sunny day,
Finding magic in the gray,
Climbing trees to touch the sky,
With every leap, I feel so spry.

Rocking rhythms in my heart,
Festive joy, a cherished art,
With each note, I smile wide,
Forever young, my spirit's guide.

Cocoon of Reflection

In soft silence, whispers bloom,
A gentle dance, freeing gloom,
Wrapped in warmth, the world fades,
Hidden thoughts in twilight wades.

Serene moments, still and bright,
Stars above, a guiding light,
Embracing dreams like precious pearls,
In this space, the spirit swirls.

Curling up in shadows' grace,
Finding peace in a quiet place,
Colors blend, a soothing hue,
Heart and soul begin anew.

Festive echoes, past and near,
As I celebrate what's clear,
A cocoon where love resides,
In reflection, joy abides.

Embracing My Shadows

In the night, a quiet call,
Shadows dance upon the wall,
Glimmers of light within the dark,
Embracing all, each hidden spark.

Woven tales of joy and pain,
Every tear holds strength to gain,
With open arms, I greet my fears,
In this moment, laughter clears.

Festive hues blend dark and bright,
A colorful soul takes flight,
Understanding in every shade,
In the shadows, dreams are laid.

So I twirl in moonlit grace,
Harmony found in the space,
Embracing what I thought was loss,
In shadows, I find my gloss.

The Garden of Self-Love

In the garden, blooms unfold,
Petals soft, a touch of gold,
Laughter sings beneath the trees,
Whispers carried by the breeze.

Nourishing roots with every thought,
Harvesting love, all fears caught,
Seeding kindness in the ground,
In this space, true joy is found.

Colors spark, a vibrant show,
Self-acceptance starts to grow,
Dancing through the fragrant air,
In my heart, I tend with care.

Festive blossoms burst in cheer,
Every ounce of love held dear,
The garden flourishes with grace,
A celebration, my own place.

Embracing the Stillness

In the quiet glow of dusk,
Laughter echoes, spirits rise,
Dancing shadows in warm light,
Underneath the starry skies.

Whispers of the night around,
Joyful hearts begin to sing,
Love wrapped softly in the sound,
Carried on the breeze of spring.

Candles flicker, shadows sway,
Each moment glimmers bright,
As the world finds its own way,
To celebrate the night.

Embrace the stillness, feel it grow,
Unite our dreams, let them flow.
With every heartbeat, every smile,
We'll treasure this moment for a while.

The Heart's Gentle Hearth

Gathered close, the warmth we share,
In a circle spun from dreams,
The laughter fills the chilly air,
As joy bursts forth in vibrant beams.

Every story, every cheer,
Brings us closer, heart to heart,
In this haven, love draws near,
From this place, we'll never part.

As the embers softly glow,
We find peace in every glance,
In the hearth, our spirits flow,
Inviting every soul to dance.

Together here, we sing our tune,
Underneath a velvet moon,
For in this space, together we start,
A festival of the humble heart.

An Echo of My Essence

In the mirror, reflections shine,
Whispers of our joy proclaim,
Each laugh, each song, a line divine,
Painting life's delightful frame.

Moments captured, gleaming bright,
Echoes of our honied past,
Carried gently through the night,
A melody that holds us fast.

In the rhythm of our embrace,
We find solace, peace restored,
In every smile, a sacred space,
Where love's true essence is adored.

With every heartbeat, every sigh,
These echoes linger, never die.
For in the dance of life we find,
The beauty woven, heart and mind.

Love's Solitary Note

A single note, a sweet refrain,
Drifts softly through the evening air,
Carried gently, like a chain,
Binding us in love's sweet care.

In a world where hearts convene,
This solitary sound takes flight,
Uniting every soul unseen,
In harmony, we greet the night.

With candles lit, we light the way,
Each flicker paints our stories bright,
In the moments where we sway,
Love's note sings beneath the light.

So let this journey be our song,
In every note, where we belong,
Together here, our spirits float,
Forever held by love's sweet note.

Self-Love's Embrace

In the mirror, I see the glow,
A smile that starts to show,
Each flaw a story, unique and bright,
In self-love's warmth, I find my light.

With every breath, I dance and sing,
Celebrating the joy I bring,
The heart that blooms, a vibrant rose,
In self-love's coat, my spirit grows.

I twirl like confetti in the air,
Embracing all that I can share,
For in this festivity, I claim my truth,
In self-love's embrace, I revel in youth.

So let the laughter fill the space,
With every beat, I find my place,
In this festival, I rise above,
Wrapped in the magic of self-love.

Holding My Heart Close

With each heartbeat, I feel the beat,
Holding my heart, a rhythmic seat,
Tender whispers in the night,
Wrapped in warmth, everything feels right.

In quiet moments, I take my time,
Savoring life in gentle rhyme,
The world outside can wait a while,
For in this love, I share a smile.

I gather moments, pure and bright,
Like fireflies that dance at night,
In the clasp of joy, I find my grace,
In holding my heart, I find my place.

With every hug, the magic swells,
In my own rhythm, my spirit tells,
A tale of joy, a melody sweet,
Holding my heart close, I feel complete.

Nestled in Solace

In quiet corners, peace unfolds,
Nestled in solace, I find gold,
Gentle breezes call my name,
In this stillness, I stake my claim.

Soft petals of dreams, they drift,
In the silence, I find my gift,
A sanctuary where I can be,
Nestled in solace, forever free.

My thoughts dance lightly, like snowflakes,
Creating joy that gently wakes,
In every heartbeat, I find the tune,
Embracing solitude, beneath the moon.

I wrap myself in soft, warm light,
A celebration of pure delight,
Nestled in solace, my soul takes flight,
In this festive peace, all feels right.

The Sanctuary of Me

In the garden of my heart, I grow,
The sanctuary of me, a vibrant show,
Each flower a thought, blooming bright,
In this space, I find pure delight.

With each petal, I learn to believe,
In the magic that I can weave,
Roots of strength, deep and wide,
In the sanctuary, I take my stride.

The colors swirl like a twirling dance,
Each moment embraced, a sweet romance,
In laughter and love, I thrive and play,
The sanctuary of me, my joyful stay.

So let the sun shine on my face,
In this haven, I find my grace,
A festival of spirit, wild and free,
In the sanctuary of me, I just be.

Anchored in Self-Acceptance

In vibrant hues, I stand so free,
Embracing all that's truly me.
With laughter bright and spirit high,
I dance like stars lit in the sky.

Each flaw a gem, each scar a tale,
On this fine journey, I will sail.
No more the weight of doubt and strife,
In joyful rhythm, I find my life.

With open arms, I greet the day,
In self-acceptance, I will sway.
The love I give reflects my mind,
In every heart, a peace I find.

Together we will raise our voice,
In unity, we'll all rejoice.
With every step, our spirits soar,
Anchored in love, we seek no more.

The Nest of My Dreams

In branches tall, a nest I weave,
A place of hope where dreams believe.
With petals soft and skies so blue,
My heart finds peace in shades of hue.

With whispers sweet, the breezes play,
In this warm nest, I choose to stay.
Where laughter sparkles, joy surrounds,
A world of wonders here abounds.

The stars above like lanterns shine,
In every shadow, love's design.
With every feather, stories tell,
In the embrace of dreams, I dwell.

Together here, we'll build and grow,
In the nest of dreams, our spirits glow.
With hearts entwined, we'll soar so free,
In this beloved home, just you and me.

A Reflective Embrace

In quiet moments, a soft embrace,
Reflections dance, and shadows trace.
With every thought that drifts away,
I find the light in shades of gray.

The joy of stillness wraps around,
In gentle peace, my heart is found.
With every sigh, I feel the grace,
In this calm pause, I find my place.

Through whispers deep, my spirit sings,
In solitude, the freedom brings.
With open arms, I greet the night,
In the embrace of stars, I find my light.

Here in the silence, wisdom plays,
A tapestry of countless days.
With every breath, I choose to flow,
In reflective stillness, love will grow.

The Silence Speaks Volumes

Amidst the noise, a hush takes flight,
The silence wraps the world so tight.
In whispers soft, the heart conveys,
The unvoiced truths of countless days.

Like gentle waves upon the shore,
In quietude, we seek once more.
With every pause, the echoes bloom,
In this still space, there's room for gloom.

Yet joy emerges from every sound,
In the void, our hopes resound.
With every glance, the soul connects,
In stillness, love reflects and respects.

So let the silence weave its song,
In harmony, where we belong.
The volumes speak, so rich, so true,
In quiet corners, I find you.

Healing Through Embrace

In the warm light of a gentle day,
Laughter blooms and worries sway.
Hearts collide, joy in the dance,
Healing whispers, given a chance.

Joyful voices lift the air,
Every moment, love to share.
Together we mend, laughter fades fears,
In each hug, a world appears.

The beat of drums, the clink of cheer,
Memories crafted, forever dear.
With each embrace, we hold the light,
Healing through love, our spirits ignite.

So let the music play on high,
Underneath the vibrant sky.
Hearts entwined in festive grace,
In the warmth of a simple embrace.

Balancing on My Own Two Feet

The sun breaks through, a brand new dawn,
Stepping forward, fears are gone.
Hypnotic rhythms flow with ease,
Balancing on dreams like leaves in breeze.

With each sway, I find my ground,
In the chaos, a joyful sound.
Heart and mind in harmony play,
Each moment a burst, come what may.

Laughter twirls in the vibrant air,
A circle of friends, a bond to share.
In this dance, I feel the heat,
Spinning freely on my own two feet.

Celebration shines in every turn,
In the magic of motion, I learn.
Each leap and bound, I'm feeling free,
In the rhythm of life, I just be.

Sanctuary of Wholeness

In the hush of twilight's glow,
Gathered close, letting feelings show.
Nature sings, a soothing balm,
In this sanctuary, hearts are calm.

Stars above twinkle with grace,
Guiding us to a sacred space.
Together we build our joyful nest,
In laughter and love, we find our rest.

Songs of old, we gently hum,
Stories shared, we all become.
Embracing the night with care,
In this wholeness, life feels rare.

Unity shines, a beacon bright,
Holding hands, we chase the light.
In this haven, pure and true,
Finding solace, me and you.

When Silence Speaks

In the calm of an endless night,
The world pauses, hearts take flight.
Silence gathers, a warm embrace,
Finding clarity in the quiet space.

Beneath the stars, thoughts align,
Whispers linger, a sacred sign.
In the hush, we hear the deep,
A shared moment, a promise to keep.

Festive hearts feel each pulse,
In stillness, our spirits convulse.
When silence speaks, joy takes flight,
In every breath, the world feels right.

Connections bloom in the still of night,
Hand in hand, we share delight.
Together we find what words can't say,
In quiet moments, love finds its way.

The Art of Self-Compassion

In the mirror, I find my grace,
Understanding dances on my face.
With gentle tones, I speak to me,
A soft embrace, I am set free.

Through storms of doubt, I raise my hand,
Each little flaw, a grain of sand.
I paint my soul with colors bright,
Embracing shadows, finding light.

A Love Letter to Me

Dear self, you are a work of art,
In every flaw, you play your part.
I cherish you, in all you do,
With every heartbeat, I love you true.

Together we'll dance through day and night,
Painting dreams in colors bright.
With tender words, I hold you near,
In every moment, I choose to cheer.

Cradled Within My Heart

A cozy nook where love abides,
In silent whispers, joy confides.
I tend the flame, so warm and right,
Cradled within, my heart takes flight.

Through laughter and tears, I find my way,
This self-love grows stronger each day.
With every step, I choose to see,
The beauty here, in being me.

Solace of Self

In quiet moments, I take a pause,
Embracing me, and all my flaws.
A soothing balm, my inner song,
In the heart's embrace, I belong.

Surrounded by love, I find my peace,
Within my soul, my worries cease.
In celebration, I stand so tall,
In the solace of self, I have it all.

The Arc of Self-Care

In the garden, laughter plays,
Colors dance in joyful rays.
Each petal whispers sweet delight,
A canvas bright, a warm invite.

Beneath the sun, we stretch and sway,
Find ourselves in the light of day.
With every breath, a vow we share,
To cherish life, to truly care.

Laughter echoes, food is spread,
With friends around, no word unsaid.
Hearts collide in a joyful tune,
Together, we rise to greet the moon.

With every smile, we paint the air,
A festival of love laid bare.
In this arc, we find our space,
A moment in life, a warm embrace.

Moments of Tranquility

Beneath the stars, the night unfolds,
Whispers of calm in shadows bold.
A distant chime, a soft caress,
In the stillness, we find our rest.

Candles flicker, shadows play,
In this haven, let worries sway.
The world outside fades from view,
As silence wraps us, pure and true.

Sipping tea, we share our dreams,
Lost in thoughts, the mind redeems.
In gentle waves, our spirits soar,
Moments of peace, forevermore.

A breath, a pause, together here,
In each heartbeat, harmony near.
With every sigh, the night unfolds,
Moments of calm, a treasure to hold.

A Cup of Inner Peace

As steam arises, warmth ignites,
A fragrant blend in cozy sights.
With every sip, the world unwinds,
In this ritual, serenity finds.

Lemon, ginger, hibiscus bright,
Each flavor mingles, pure delight.
In the quiet, thoughts take flight,
A cup of peace, a sweet respite.

Friends gather round, sharing joy,
Laughter and stories we employ.
In clinking cups, our spirits cheer,
Together we toast, the day draws near.

With gratitude wrapped in each taste,
We savor moments, never haste.
In this blend, our hearts release,
A simple joy, a cup of peace.

Through My Own Window

Colors splash, the world a show,
Through my window, life does glow.
Children laughing, skies so blue,
Every moment feels brand new.

Seasons change, a dance of light,
From dawn's blush to starry night.
Fragrant blooms in springtime's grace,
Through my window, I find my place.

Leaves a-fall, a golden hue,
In soft whispers, the winds pursue.
Each frame a story, life alive,
Through my window, I truly thrive.

Snowflakes twirl in winter's embrace,
In the quiet, I find my pace.
Through every glance, the beauty grows,
In my own world, peace overflows.

Whispered Reverie

In twilight's glow, laughter ignites,
With dancing lights, the heart takes flight.
Balloons afloat, a rainbow display,
Joyful moments, come what may.

Around the table, stories are shared,
In the warmth of love, none are spared.
With every cheer, our spirits soar,
Together we stand, forevermore.

Sweet melodies drift on the breeze,
Echoing laughter among the trees.
Celebration whispers through the night,
A tapestry woven, pure delight.

As stars peek down, we raise our glass,
To fleeting moments that swiftly pass.
With hearts entwined, our souls embrace,
In this whispered reverie, we find our place.

Wrapped in My Resilience

Wrapped in warmth, a vibrant glow,
Embracing dreams that softly flow.
With every setback, I rise anew,
In festive spirit, I'm bold and true.

The world may sway, but I stand tall,
With laughter bright, I conquer all.
In every challenge, I find my core,
Wrapped in strength, I seek to soar.

Colors burst, like fireworks in flight,
In every heartbeat, I find the light.
Together we gather, hand in hand,
In the warmth of love, forever we stand.

With a smile that shines, I greet the day,
In resilience wrapped, I'll find my way.
With joy unbound, I celebrate,
In this festive moment, I elevate.

Solitary Strength

In quiet corners, strength resides,
In solitude, my spirit glides.
With every breath, I find my peace,
In whispered thoughts, my worries cease.

The world around may rush and race,
But in stillness, I find my place.
A festive heart beats strong and true,
In shadows deep, I bloom anew.

As candles flicker, shadows dance,
In solitude, I take my chance.
To celebrate the light within,
In silent joy, my soul begins.

With every moment, strength I gain,
In solitude, I lose my pain.
Embracing life with open arms,
In solitary strength, I find my charms.

The Touch of Inner Peace

In gentle whispers, calm prevails,
Through soft caresses, love unveils.
A festive spirit, bright and true,
In every heartbeat, I renew.

With tranquil breaths, I find my way,
In peaceful moments, I long to stay.
The world may whirl, yet I remain,
In inner peace, I feel no pain.

As laughter echoes, joy takes flight,
In golden hues of soft twilight.
A touch of solace, sweet and light,
In every heartbeat, pure delight.

I dance with grace, surrendering strife,
In the rhythm of the festive life.
With open arms, I greet the dawn,
In the touch of peace, my fears are gone.

Embers of Inner Warmth

Amidst the glow of flickering light,
Laughter dances, spirits take flight.
Cherished moments, a joyful sight,
In the heart's embrace, everything feels right.

Glasses clink, a toast to cheer,
Whispers of love, we hold so dear.
Friends and family, gathered near,
In the warmth of this festive sphere.

The fire crackles, stories unfold,
Memories shared, like treasures of gold.
With every smile, our hearts are bold,
In this tapestry, our lives are rolled.

As shadows dance and stars appear,
The night ignites, filled with good cheer.
In the embers' glow, we draw near,
A celebration of love very clear.

Layers of Reflection

Pieces of laughter, scattered around,
Layers of joy in every sound.
Moments unfold as we gather 'round,
In the tapestry of love profound.

Glimmers of memories touch our hearts,
Each shared glance, a work of art.
In the spirit of festivity, we take part,
Binding our souls, never to part.

With every story, we stitch anew,
Threads of connection in every hue.
Celebrating life, it's all we pursue,
In the dance of time, we're never through.

The night blossoms, a radiant sight,
With laughter echoing into the night.
Together we stand, in joy's light,
Our hearts forever sparkling bright.

Wandering My Thoughts

In the quiet moments, reflections bloom,
Thoughts wander softly, dispelling the gloom.
Amidst the festivities, there's room,
For dreams to flourish, finding their loom.

Images dance like fireflies' flight,
Carried on breezes, soft and light.
Voices entwined, echoes of delight,
In this celebration, hearts take flight.

Bubbles of laughter rise in the air,
Joyful connections, moments we share.
The essence of life, we handle with care,
In the web of togetherness, love is rare.

As I wander, my thoughts intertwine,
With each pulse of joy, our spirits align.
In the realm of festivity, we shine,
Embracing the magic, so divine.

The Embrace of Now

In the embrace of now, we find our place,
A tapestry woven with love's grace.
Time pauses gently, a warm embrace,
As we gather in this jubilant space.

Peals of laughter ring out clear,
Moments of bliss, we hold so dear.
In the glow of joy, there's nothing to fear,
United in love, our hearts steer.

The clock ticks softly, yet we abide,
In the magic of here, where dreams collide.
With every heartbeat, there's much to confide,
In this festive blanket, we take pride.

As stars twinkle and candles gleam,
Let's cherish each heartbeat, each shared dream.
In the embrace of now, we redeem,
The spirit of joy, like a flowing stream.

Serenity's Cradle

In the glow of the lantern's light,
Joyful whispers take their flight.
Stars twinkle like playful eyes,
As laughter mingles with night's sighs.

The soft breeze carries sweet delight,
Children giggle in pure delight.
Colors twirl in the dusky air,
Each moment is a chance to share.

Music dances with the trees,
Floating softly on the breeze.
Hearts unite in warm embrace,
Finding beauty in this place.

Underneath the moon's soft gaze,
Time slows down, in a gentle haze.
Together, we create our dreams,
In serenity's cradle, it seems.

A Dance with Myself

In the mirror, I see the light,
Waves of joy take their flight.
Swirling skirts in vibrant hues,
A dance of rhythm, no need for shoes.

The music plays, my heart takes lead,
Every twirl, a spirit freed.
Footsteps echo on the floor,
A celebration, forevermore.

With every spin, I shed my cares,
Laughter floats in the evening airs.
In this moment, I feel alive,
In a dance, my soul will thrive.

With each beat, I find my place,
Embracing joy, a sweet embrace.
This dance, my heart's delight,
A journey shines in the night.

Shadows that Comfort

In the twilight, shadows play,
Flickering lights lead the way.
Each silhouette softly sways,
Dancing along through the haze.

Underneath the starlit dome,
We find solace, a sense of home.
Whispers linger in the air,
A gentle balm for every care.

Hand in hand, the world feels bright,
As we waltz into the night.
Nature hums a lullaby,
Echoing dreams beneath the sky.

These shadows wrap us, soft as lace,
Creating warmth in a tranquil space.
Together we revel, side by side,
In shadows that comfort, we abide.

Tapestry of Self

Threads of color, woven tight,
Stories shared in soft moonlight.
Every stitch a tender memory,
Creating art, a tapestry.

With vibrant dreams, we intertwine,
Each heartbeat a sparkling line.
Together, we celebrate our truth,
Embracing wonders of our youth.

In the fabric, warmth resides,
Unity where each heart abides.
A kaleidoscope of joy on view,
Each thread a bond, forever true.

Through every laugh, through every tear,
The tapestry grows, year by year.
A celebration of who we are,
In this woven world, we shine like stars.

www.ingramcontent.com/pod-product-compliance
Ingram Content Group UK Ltd.
Pitfield, Milton Keynes, MK11 3LW, UK
UKHW030847221224
452712UK00006B/443

9 789908 125480